Excursions
by Gordon Carrega

Excursions
© 2015 by Gordon Carrega (carrega@gmx.de)
Photos by Ursula Schorn. Design by Petra Reisdorf
Published by Books on Demand GmbH, Norderstedt
Printed in Germany
ISBN: 9783734774577

CONTENTS

 7 The Calling
 8 Think So
 9 At Liberty
10 Plans
11 Take Me Take Me Take Me
12 Time Out
13 Where Are We Now
14 Vague Now
19 Excursions
29 Difference Between the Spoken
30 Come Now
36 Strategies
48 Knell
49 Sources
50 Beneath the Archway
51 Look What You
52 What I like About You
53 Once Again
54 Mostly
55 Transit Sequence
58 Tracts
62 Enclosures
74 Imago

Gordon Carrega lives in Berlin, Germany. He has published four previous collections of prose poems, **Back Gate, A Place to Stay, Life of the Party,** and **Up Ahead.**

"Please bear in mind that the exit might be behind you."

Instructions from the flight attendant

THE CALLING

you've got to be here
to tell a story
we wait at the gate
the gate of ashes

time always taken
burning down the road
all we're saying
same direction

voices heard
which lead to never
the calling indeed
has come to call

*

the distance
taking pains

the measure
can be taken

all the ways
and none

the well planned ruins
as a story
takes its form

*

how pure
the reconnaissance
of what will never
take place

THINK SO

think so
therefore you are
here with me

gathering postcards
the quality we call
the future

from now on
always a sometime thing
not anymore than you
delving into frequency

while holding the key
to elsewhere
all the time on earth
round every bend

AT LIBERTY

sitting it out in the timeworn
to verify what's never once again
waiting knows you more
at liberty to include

as much as oblivion given
after has you in place
the game is sprung
a continual lurking
when and where in one mouthful
a word at a word
to face the particulars

*

listening to the end in thunder
constancy of nobody else
one by one shedding light
shedding darkness
the interior half
of what's the other half
the art of zero times
the same zero times
offered to never

never succeeds
the mirror for somebody
eternal leave of absence

PLANS

that it's everybody's
having and not having
possessed equally
forever has already happened

just as forgetting is a function
or meaning to say
sleeping is always a was thing
or wondering just what you're

supposed to look like as they're all
singing happy birthday
requires participation
one thing in place of another
until there's nothing left
in understanding why

the known conditions
feeling right at home
as someone coming in suddenly
with the look of a messenger
the hand of course reaches
its crafty design in the thin air

TAKE ME TAKE ME TAKE ME

Someone speaks up, someone writes it all down, someone takes a holiday, someone screams, "Am I supposed to wait? Am I supposed to ask? Is this some kind of character study? Is this an occupation? It feels like an occupation. Am I now in your shoes?"

Heaven helps those who helps themselves. This, you see, is dinner at eight. You may sit right here beside me. Tonight's the night. One thing follows another as we anticipate big branches to swing on. Lacking as we do a sense of location to clear up a few misunderstandings.

The letter that came back. Sudden laughter. Everyone in the audience. Everyone in the audience got lost.

TIME OUT

the number of fingerprints you decided to introduce
in soft focus with those perfect swirls of character
t'was a real convention so I wandered off
to be obscure and reminisce

a contentment neither voluptuous nor sublime
but one of these days I'll get it right
from beginning to end in full color glossy photos
like everyone else with their theatrical aspirations
and bicycles which they eagerly wheel indoors

thank you thank you for bringing your English racer in here with you
for I am thrilled by the nervousness of waiting for a sign
to turn into glitter like spokes in the hot sun
but in the meantime I am no less fortunate
as I continue to hear the sirens and the falling leaves
that are so much heavier this year

but not to be mistaken for the perfect moment
watching the mouth of a dog opening to bark
and it's all so terribly familiar

WHERE ARE WE NOW

who do you mean looks like
save your graces
friends at the club

cause matter purpose
this fleshy frame may feel
driven to same yesterday

attitude like a feather
vie for the season
our journal exists from the time

what to anticipate
what word works harder than not
this is indeed the path that leads

or simply the path itself
one version a page with columns
a floating line

the mind at prayer
whether the same is the same
that pile of leaves over there

what pile of leaves over where
think back before the wind
you must mean imagine

VAGUE NOW

enough of never
gestures to anticipate

a shade equal
to the given

we've seen this part
last of its kind

*

the glare since when
measures up
the first to know

known in common
the incomplete

if not the way
the eyes deal
out the time

*

since too late
if an ending
seems random

length of stay
elsewhere
else entirely

meaning to
round it all off
the other hand
in thin air

*

learned distance
completes no end
to completion

an echo someplace

the news to start out
between one never
or another

combined to fall away

duration deposits delay

appearances chalked up

*

day seen to
takes the play

if only runs
time between

only one
what runs

what's not
one knows

in range

*

from as in
or another
to join

at intervals
as a way of
from as in

or another
given to
give what

shall we
something in
as empty

complete does
it say from
as in a place

here empty
so you can
already does

it say joined
at intervals
a series to tell

what shall we
of tendency
on all sides

to intend a view

*

looking to forget
with what besides

though just
right where
ashes as one
does to prosper

*

any attribute
starts out
not to become other

sheer presence
one would isolate
to continue

entirely as
the hand waving
to include the forgotten

*

here as well
to see why
or not the look

in your eye
looks back
includes loss

a ploy by chance
from before
to serve

gestures freely
spinning shades

well acquainted
one who frequents
of long standing

into the word

imitate late
closed door
camouflage

to forget again
acquires rhythm

gravity

*

the way smoke
hand over hand
even the same

again hereafter

*

called to answer
etched in particulars

out of number
at one time

one silence
from now

intervals of never
within call

EXCURSIONS

we can return
later it seems
the schedule
a few weeks

we must
prepare
how much
time
is
let's go
into
it

some of us
left earlier
traveling without haste
owing to the early start

in the direction
previously agreed upon

*

you come to a place
history was once sudden
an eerie half-light
what's mostly visible
from where we know

we have to live here you know
the constant research
halfway into the woods
halfway out
meet me halfway

the dye cast
dialogue fashioned
held in time
timely
the claim held
though mostly circumstantial

*

possessed by motive
just as you are
a bell rang

so many train windows
before the finale
under the spell
a particular weakness

something simple like thunder
pages beneath the weight of opera
the troops had already left
a few letters in the meantime

were they permanent
a horse in the courtyard
all that is precious
a clearer light in here
the same impulses

more discreet and kind
the wind comes closer
knock on any door.

*

all familiar
which helped the design
composed against
nothing of equivalence
when regarded as your entry

the scheme for the asking
style as it was known or expected
effort to place the scale
quite accurately a reaching toward

to know around you
messages suitable for the occasion
as you came in
on time as usual

*

everybody's idea
of a success
right there in the room
close enough
nowhere else
this guy beside me

there was no one
actually a mere idea
we fall back on our mistakes
you see I thought there were
others or another
rather to add credence

the box I sent just
today in the mail
oh that was then it was
empty but I have
paid my dues
quite long enough

we count the losses
what against them
can we hold up

*

there was after all
a schedule you followed
with some purpose
later you realize
through absence
of what had continually appeared

a few things came to an end
history precedes solitude
blessings of the familiar
cast upon what passes
simple ruins upon the land
held fact and theory

some new beginnings
we return to a place
let's see what there is
in terms only of differences
face to face what's done then
mask then no more

*

right where you left off
earlier in the week
certainly what's expected
got here before you
remember now
the schedule afterwards
the going what's taken
at first completion
in the original

get there on time
pick up the key
give ourselves
of ourselves
what was it now
after daybreak
at the last minute
the daily aspect
the end result

you of all people
all the way back
let's find a way
let's find a target
to make it possible
this time for sure
in perspective

to look is one thing
to disappear in a crowd
the faces already searched
something about choice
being chosen
let me see now
to engage each other
gearing up I heard lately

you can't help it
turned out to be
the same in a way
a project to be undertaken
a lifetime of effort
a chilling effect
up to date
it suits you

*

the applause
clear as day
we can recall
the audience
rose to their feet

let's set the scene
as we planned
coordinate the flashbacks
with the interruptions
a whole series
before your very eyes
the actions of others
those you know

get us through at times
let's be finally
a somebody
from where you're standing
let's be timeless
on the look out

how it was
it's a little late now
let's file a report
as best we can
let's have a look
like you think it is
on your own

you've come the distance
the best laid plans
from the outset
from the outside
looking in
it looks good
we gather strength
for what it takes
let's count the days
there in the offing

*

was a place
some kind of place
the news
coming in
we couldn't stop it
we might have wanted to

the news kept
coming in
like from everywhere
we made sense of it
then it didn't matter
everything was happening
at the same time

*

to find myself amidst
so many others
going in the same direction
let's greet each day

I might not understand
exactly what you're saying
but I'm sure you mean it
either way I'm drawn
to whatever there is between us

to know what you did
when you did
basis this particular
holds its ground
more than you know
somehow the usual case

*

what was waiting one step in this direction
what had to be there already
in the service of forgetting
I used to tell you based on a story
the scheduled sameness the same schedule
the same time on schedule
was really something
could never be otherwise
in the service of memory
what was there already
vague though it is
there were no moments anymore

*

is there a sign
the usual keys
call if you're late

the light in here
you belong completely
the piano arrived

common errors
the dog barked all night
the door closed

your small courage
your civilities
mention the roses
arriving on the bells

the same story
kept us occupied
raking leaves
a windy afternoon

*

the impression of having arrived
this into seeming memory
a pact with always
it all turns out
make a dream come true
the last breath

the one that's waiting
up ahead or far behind
oh it's you again
I remember now
calling for completion
at center stage
complete remembering
if you is said
for one unending loss

*

one sound just like the other
after all this time
to make a difference
where we begin or leave off
here I am with the crowd in the background
a milestone
watch it disappear
every inch of ground for all the world
for all we know
gets done or gets said

direction at all costs we can rely on
closing in
weight of impermanence
not just any silence
your silence
a gesture to make a point
earlier reference just in case
a summary a doorway
with nothing
a flag a profile the open window sky
pure dialect to know one another

*

the ways we have come
content to achieve its own axis
how we prepared
the series of preparation
exemplified the best way
the turn of events

the aftermath
the location
we keep looking to explain
exactly what is still held
a chorus finally within the storm

DIFFERENCES BETWEEN THE SPOKEN

Lonesome mystic. Lost static. Duration of current states of mind and events. No family to speak of. A brand new urge. Getting all dressed up. Brute necessity. Consistent with uncertainty. You seem to be back already. Moving void between lips.

A name for whatever happens. Dead weight desire. Wretched contentment. A world of shadows. Whisperings. Observation disturbs a result that exists in and for. Gray bridge gray water gray sky gray bird gray smoke. Please repeat the question.

Impartial chaos. The rains came. A set of basic feelings. Still you're different with different people. Compare compare appear with disappear. The only reason you don't remember is because you forgot. The point at which parallels meet. Topic sentence.

Action speaks in tongues. The blind date keeps happening. Explanations are provisional yet they multiply. No time to call home. Time in a different place all the time. Time in by the time he died. Time in a forest of hats. Time casually slumped in an offhand moment.

COME NOW

to intimate what your blindness knows
we say shown because making a gesture
on any given day the unseen
gestures to amend
the daily hint at story

*

each word in front of itself
advances an alibi
does pattern being varied
between seeing
transition in place
when is always horizon

*

the many layers silence contains
to reconcile what hasn't happened
lays bare shadow
how much is how much has to be
shadow into shadow goes real time
at face value

*

now is making the inevitable
to partake
gets the idea
same look equals same
looking to arrive

*

the actual depth
through gaps in space
the perspective
wrested from the actual
to know is not always

*

"I'm back."
"We all are."
what in other
words in what
other words

*

frame was self
satisfied in being
exactly that frame
that frame was
the flock flew through
the frame
one standard sufficed
calling direction to each
thereby adding passage to occur

*

what more could afford
us entry what more entry
could be afforded
because of the angle

told to take our time
in the general scope
of what seemed certain
quite satisfied the well constructed tale
permission granted to walk across
looking for the bird song in occupy
the flair in signature

days falling off
no sound at all
unlike any known silence
more or less refusing to be underlined

*

one way to one side
given effects
a boundary
today hides the day
instance
outline
routine
want to wanting
shore becomes
coastline

*

taken in the being taken over
must needs be we keep telling ourselves
the narrative of the told self

*

command cuddling up
with choice while the next
instance turns up elsewhere

drenched in the floodlights
the footman casts no shadow

*

self-evident
the weight of a gaze
all in all today
your want conformed
to your own image

*

eyeballing space
in a series
tubular
seamless
speaks well
the inclination to endurance
amounting to
an impelling force
a large part of what's meant
by meaning it
that which can be seen
remaining visible

*

away leaves off
knowing is more
or less leaning
the dark has weight against the air

*

a step taken
verging upon half a reason
matching up with
half a reason
identical with
what happens

*

the same
creaking hinge
the expert
wanting a closer look

too up close
no longer in sight
the norm
the right place
rule of thumb

some warm-ups
broadly to get ready
save the last dance
just save it
one does

go from
here to there
to come back
might or might
not be to return

*

applause kept
ghosts mediate
the quick of it
a turn in taking
each plus every
to keep up
night replaces
kinds of night

*

something to win
adds up to knowing
no sooner said
I came from
that direction
you just have to point
and the view changes

*

memory committed
to memory
familiar scrawl
foggy night

no dice
no tight-rope
between a reason
and a meaning

the last gasp
coming up wanting
wanting more

STRATEGIES

1/

Up the long familiar path. Home again for the weekend. A summary to precede the flashback as gradually a perspective emerges where earlier there had been merely complaint in line with what is often called the future.

Oh how this cataloging has kept us on schedule, one of which, a schedule, is always kept within reach to ease the inquiries. The reunion came about on the return trip to retrieve the binoculars.

A thorough sense of exactly this location more than any other sums up the music in such a way that no recollection is possible against the chill. It could have been you quoted a student of pure research as choices burnt their shadows in the summons.

Give me time in some refuge, the slow grace between question and response. A a satisfaction without legend. Hardly a race, hardly a quarrel, hardly an attitude or a sense of style.

2/

Memories of a most relaxing occasion. Everybody must be somewhere at a given time, haunting the backstage.

You wrought your will, strengthened under the existing forms and honor paid. Filling everything with your very presence common to all of us at least for the moment in the memory to test fitness.

Learn from what is done, though questions tend to jump out in many directions. Run for the bus, have dinner ready. None other who works for you, sweeping the sidewalk every morning.

Brilliant. Funny, gifted, tragic, off-beat, you make everything which is made, isolated in its very perfection. Considering the possible link, based primarily it seems on what has been so far discovered. Adding to our body of knowledge. Or to speak more honestly, one continuous mistake.

3/

If you just go on proper as should be. If you perform the first action with enough quality of scope to fully satisfy those among us who wait for the results coming in.

Take what you can, the various outlines of the urge to live admirably. Your virile common sense summing it all up right from the start. To endure is more than I know, being always more than the obvious.

See me just this way and now just that way. It's a very rare thing indeed, more slowness than memory, more silhouette than ever. Ask me and I'll tell you.

And what if you on purpose had chosen tomorrow instead of today would a clearer light in here show us more fully as I ponder my generous wish to share with you all that is precious, to occupy and inspire? Speaking totally from experience, no gushing forth nor preliminaries. While a question turns in the air and begins its return.

4/

Hey there tossed about in the original! Everyone's waiting back there where you came from. Want to go back? Working from memory or whatever passes for a lie detector test? At the very end, yes you use your eyes. Like suddenly wanting to register doubt. Coming or going one sees what one means.

Earlier the fortunate blaring on city streets, two fire engines sirens at full blast speeding in opposite directions. Never write down your dreams unless haunted by lack of foresight.

How to save our necks from that which right now is passing? You won't be here tomorrow. OK. you will be here but in two weeks, going off to take photos of the pyramids. What then? That's the thing of it, immersed in conditions.

Walking towards each other, the tour operator calls out names. He says applause, he says reason. He saw a lion once from what only moments before had been pure backdrop. Hearing the news against what passes for structure when you're still in it for the money.

5/

Shadowed in the dim unsatisfactory dependence on chance. Often you're early. It's not serious. Sometimes you call at the last minute.

People talk endlessly. People stay late. This here's the straight line, the reasonable assurances. Don't spend more than you need to.
A standard against which the large, intensely desired best possible offering, if once performed satisfactorily likely to be called upon again.

Everything falling more and more into place. Another perfect neck-sized iron ring carefully labeled necessity one hundred and wherever you are in the counting demands of fate. And you without your tools.

Obscure with shoes on, a passing fancy. This here's the key, the gracious, precise, well-fondled. And over there, slightly to the left of the piano, that's where we'll put the dead, I mean the deed, when it comes through the door.

6/

You're playing all the parts, good at what you do. "One of the lucky ones," someone says. Then things settle down a bit. The way things happen, a ritual that surprises you. Not like you think it would. Self-satisfied given your background.

And of course you weren't there which spoiled things a bit for the rest of us. No one complained. Sharing in your absence, the sun grew hot. There was a brief wait at the gate. You can well imagine. Wishing you had come brought out the best in everyone, the wish one means, the wish did this.

You must stop and think, develop your way of seeing, take notes. You could help us remember with questions carefully chosen from the permanent collection. Put yourself in someone else's place just this once. The last time we discussed it, you gave the impression of uncertainty. A sign of intelligence.

The names had been changed but we knew the answer from when memory had been committed on these trails. See that smoke over there on the hillside? Not that hillside. Look at where we're pointing. That's it, that hillside.

7/

You know the way you old storyteller with plans for the next outing to the memorial. Face of someone you know but you don't know who. Let's face it you're talking to me. You must be talking to me. There's nobody else here.

A space in the world filled only by you. Strut your stuff out one door and in the next. End product of an otherwise internal process. Covers a lot of ground and attitude as usual. Who's the guy with courage of convictions lettered all over himself? The same fellow who's always asking to take a look at the map. As you were going in he was coming out.

A web of mutual interests. Obligations getting the best of us. Then the dream, then the capacity to dream more or less dominated the landscape. And of course someone's always stealing the original, to re-live, as you have always suspected, the experience.

8/

Memory you say. You say plans, looking forward. It's like that echo, that shadow. Keep a diary. One day it will become a book. Such things happen at the right time. Preserving the first person. Suffering the immediacy. Holding a candle. Sifting the evidence.

The glossy photos. Whole chains of circumstances lying around all day awaiting your return. Clearly understood as we lurk about, tugging at the edges for a better view. Keep in mind this might be the right time. Simply stated, you might be waiting, you might be missing, you might still be relevant though invisible.

And yet the time comes when it must be said you were not in the same place at the same time as much as the other guy who's truly contemporary while you're merely on your way to send postcards. One day you'll come back and it will be just like yesterday, even if right now you're traveling unseen in a series of episodes.

It is our nature to wonder, to recognize to call out and be heard. The continual prospects set in our path though we are among strangers. The sky in the old days, it all came to nothing.

9/

You can usually tell beforehand but still too late to make a difference. Yet you regret nothing. You remember now there was a young man and he spoke just those words before he played his tune which betrayed him. There were wings, familiar to all, and we refused him.

The refusal carried you as in uplifted, turning away as in strengthened. To be caught in this position one has to get here. You got here, didn't you? If things could be any different then they would be. Like all the others who have come before, you tend to take too much responsibility. Slack off a bit. It has come to pass.

"You can trust me," someone said, frowning in that particular way, haunted by self doubt. So very different from the other guy. Just yesterday as you were enjoying the view, he stepped right up and said, "That's my window through which you're now looking." And you knew for sure he meant it.

10/

The captivity of a fine example as you are to interpretation under the usual sway of circumstances. Polish the lamp and trim the wick. Rake about on the scrap of garden.

A certain form has been composed. Evokes by association the sensation of a definite inner content. The eternal present with impartial observation. A simple human cry for satisfaction in such pure weather. Same dreary waves breaking. Exclusive large true facts from birth of wish and purpose.

What remains in you still untouched by the passage like the rest of us lighthouse keepers. As far as you can remember this time a year ago you had similar genuine concerns. Your immediate surroundings were the same where there used to be your neighbor in the aftermath of what's come and gone.

11/

The body in memory returns with a force of endearing proportions. Whose body? Let's get it right this time. Let's make it to the end. Through the park to the museum. Shadows on the wall at the museum, the white wall, as the guide explained or talked a lot. A real harbinger he was, solemn action itself.

The patrol went out, missed signals or something else entirely. The lost patrol. We had spoken all about it a short while ago when I agreed to see everything in a different light just because you said so. But how about a total lack of emphasis all the way to the end, a total lack, a lack of total emphasis.

Why always this craze about the end? Who's going somewhere, who will write to us, will go on to describe, will remember. We've already worked out the details, a gift saying you belong, saying be at home, saying allow a variety of light, sound, the space of being. A kind of guesswork that turns out fine for all concerned.

12/

Always where you've always been. Coming in daily you must be an ending, a cause, a satisfaction you get in return. The last time I saw your face. At the same time we give everything, we empty ourselves.

If not now, if not when to verify the clinging temporary within which we look further into the appearances to be known through which the shadows, whispering to us from the afterlife, follow our language all the way back to the first word.

And there used to be just you on any given day. Meeting someone or not meeting someone, you stand between the very recognition at the first of the line, the ideal setting.

We returned home in the evening delighted to discuss the sequences that had brought us through, to instruct others where meant to be.

KNELL

Something goes boom in the distance and all the pigeons scatter. But the rest of us we continue. The statue casts its large shadow. You don't have to understand it or anything essential. I feel the same today as I did yesterday when I stayed home sick in bed but today I'm rearing to go.

Muddy shoes on the white carpet. How tactless! But lucky for us it's a small, well-kept scenario, and it's grand to be here. Sun and shade cooperating excellently. A most unexpected occurrence, camera dropped upon the anvil. Oh zoom lens! Another hasty departure.

You don't have to phone. The last one to see him alive. The last one to see him dead. Dear diary, I am your servant and when I serve you, I serve you right. It serves you right, the darkness said.

Roots behind thine eyes, you with your stories neatly typed. Because you're mine, the darkness said. I don't take you necessarily seriously, but take you I will certainly take you. I don't charge extra.

One morning a man carrying a shovel, a brand new sparkling shovel, gets on the bus. And the next morning, in a completely different part of the city, the same man gets on the bus with the same shovel and it's still brand new, sparkling clean, not a scratch to indicate usage, and our human friend none the worse for wear.

And the third morning, believe me when I tell you, different location but the same man, same shovel still unused. How do you know it's the same damn shovel? He could have a whole collection. Oh a smile for every occasion, is it? Except this time his eyes meet mine as he exits the bus and I peer through the bus window. Oh God, I hate bus windows.

SOURCES

Some people like to pick it all up together just because they can take it all in one trip, but how about taking one little piece at a time, so many times, a sense of the task at hand, down the corridor and back again and down the corridor...

Trees in the wind. The usual scraps of guitar make it to the top while others just continue, their exertion, a blessing well-disguised. Yes there is a rather wide field out there, a view you might say with steeple above it all, quite the authority, you know, sky.

Where are your shorts and tennis racquet, your red sports car? Come on, join the program. Nice day to revisit the hometown and one more just like you sent back by return mail. The personality gets even more vaguely involved with the surroundings. Next time you bring the ladder.

Didn't forget the key on the table, did you? Thank God it's where you left it, and rather more ominous than I recalled from my last visit. You wouldn't think an object of such menacing aspect could do something simple like open a door.

Hush, blowing up a storm. The way you just repeat everything the next instant back at me. I love your mouth. I never think of your ears' oracular yearnings. I hang on emphasis, innuendo I never knew existed or am able to figure out.

And all this in wildflowers, and a strong wind that would already have toppled over the bench were it not for the weight of the two of us. I'm glad you agree

BENEATH THE ARCHWAY

Everything is real smooth until you start fussing around
with a name for our archway beneath which we are always sitting
and immediately I regret having agreed
in the first place to include the archway
but it seemed so historical amidst the cigar smoke
and so much better than memory
and better than either ambition or humility.
It gives us location while the October evening
insinuates its various tenses, departures, arrivals.

I appreciate how you want to be someone sensible,
how you have learned in several languages to say
"The archway, the archway."
If you want to settle for Welcome Restraint, I'll vote for that.
Do you feel more luminous now?
Does your potential want to climb on a horse?
I won't complain.
I know how to sit still and take dictation.
I know how to watch a leaf fall
and I know how to observe all that goes lurking about unnoticed.

Certainly we don't need to sink into the glaring quality
which means THIS IS IT.
But instead you might ask, "What are all these urges
for research and explanations?" as a means of moving
our conversation steadily along
and surely there is no escaping
that you have arrived often enough,
have built a correspondence on which we can depend
even though my devotion borders on excess
beyond taste or fire or fruit of the season.

LOOK WHAT YOU

thought you'd just
few minutes past
all in all

as to one or more
light in the window
shadow exited
the time being

*

you like afterwards
each place like never

orienting yourself
the question

where
may arise

*

a deeply rooted stare
in the name of

the name for
presence

the passing minute's
equal possession

nothing in hand
without the daily

just at home in death wish
or what would death wish for

WHAT I LIKE ABOUT YOU

We were together back then, traveling, you know history loves company. Takes a while to understand the art which often disintegrates in the final analysis but who sticks around that long? This or that comrade trying to get back in touch with you, sheer logistical muddle.

The world is too much with us, big thick black arrow pointing down at you, right above your head, visible to no one in particular. No questions in anybody's mind in light of the most recent failures. We rarely stayed home, reached the end and kept going.

Blazing despair? You must mean sunlight. Of course you never have the right apparel but everybody gets somewhere on the tide. You went away and came back. Tickets to the game. The past put to use. You think I wasn't but I was waiting for the right signal to blend into overture. Down the track or coming back. Never the same way twice.

In case the phone rings it rings in case you're home. Another fact discarded, like apple blossoms at the outdoor cafe, left out in the rain, swept under the rug and you're still dancing. Why don't you dance all over me? I'm not talking directly to you. It's your red high heel shoes I'm undressing. It's survival, those black wings in your basket at the start of a new day. Or thumbing through the pages of your haiku collection, no cause for alarm.

ONCE AGAIN

the more
what happens
keep at it

hat in hand
pure subject
you had to

be there
not enough
yet complete

laid bare
at the basis
the given

territory
one set
of foot prints

MOSTLY

absence at home in a voice
going all the way back
a claim on the future

knocking at the door
here and elsewhere
lurking in the shadows
had I known you were coming

these days aren't these days no more
saying is as sayings says
voice exceeding voice
a sanctuary
of insistent pleasures
don't tread on my territory

pages torn up just the other night
puzzlement between gain and loss

ghost of a chance that argued
motives for the story staked out
not this not that may flourish

TRANSIT SEQUENCE

early enough
go that way
most recent breeze
at least for the moment
this big you have to picture it
case someone was to ask
what you most expect
contained in its variety
leaning into particular silence
shape itself given

*

some quick response
to deduce a whole new set of influences
days full and various
ahead of the game
the thin air
waiting closely on the heels
including chance
the next was over
a backdrop
a nice finish
the radiance surrounding
some imminent thing or quality

*

someone's speaking
that cannot be otherwise
we came across
surface to surface
for now the reach
organized beyond
as is more was endless
to shape each excess
recognized materials
at hand
the lay of the land
time
voice
measure where most clearly seen

*

alert
resonance
a moment's notice
directly overhead
prevailing winds
memory as before
stages unbeknownst
one thing next to another
framed reference
the last one to see
the face belonging
the last one
walking back

*

the particulars discourse
resonant likeness
going in view
the same one
into another
a day
significance
assembled
gradually
activity preoccupied
the next move
a glimpse
previously caught
perfect for the story
was just this way this place
someone else comes along

*

the known path
this face just a face
we get there
the bell in time
the recurring
it's just waiting
qualifies as usual
the juncture
don't go back on us
lyrics
places

TRACTS

the expect from here you are
all encounters to establish

loss abides all around
consuming time

necessary oblivion as one is

*

act to discover before the song the song before
all ablaze to accomplish

a hand waves from here
threshold shifts
over abyss
presumed in place

has to be located
intended at the time

*

names speak
knowing in likelihood
familiar shadow
to that when passes
the invited through here
who are like us

*

went on about
known on account
of its own enough

a singular time
evidence bound like a guest
you can go if you want

*

discourse of occupations
contained distance without likeness

a walking toward
as seen before

someone speaks from occasion
once for

*

is now daily
I would understand
in the bargain
the face right in front
does what it does
an asking
as we are to become

*

history of value and effort
to appear understood
exactness was a time
vision as far as
gives the given
upon what passes
in the veryness
to find a way

*

used to the way
in your own time
pursuing against the said
to know what must
in constancy
for here I came

*

once for all
outcome constitutes a reference
serving the gain
likeness to speak of the useful
events turn as if to escape
consumes disappearance

*

arranged in certain
to attend being caught up
illumined since circumstance
be recognized as to the pure inclination
beyond what in a general direction
the lack thereof

*

which words have known to us of absence
ceremonies due the very voice on the verge
to time as to place
shadows memory

*

the given as well as a life free
a spell cast on difference we held proportionate
in case what needed was to be

*

shadows were others
all the similar quality
to witness of always
to rely us more elsewhere
future diversions
left over from when
hungry to identify the same

*

still remains surfaces
flight of a known tune
this waiting kept
in the recognition
to turn to

*

alone as if time discovers
in this to rely
already wanting condition
at the entrance the cue is heard

*

in addition the chance beyond the anecdote
the will upon activity
terms to discover
references in a chronicle
a place at least is understood
a step taken
unseen by anyone
verging upon both ways
made music

*

an end known
memory as to nature
a hand in reaching
thoroughly as cloud

ENCLOSURES

enclosure one

camera on the ladder aimed at the door
come in and do it again that is as many
abundance of motive assurance of the stripped and strapping bursting
                                        with juices not on your
                              life but simply
                      on ceremony
     a call from the beyond stopped the drum roll
          bird fell from sky
               grayness of flag and then face
at the window rain on the windowpane tears on the face either way
yours for the taking

enclosure two

a certain distance return mail a natural
conclusion resulted
personal fruitless at windows
buckets on the stairs the inspired life
a guiding principle tucked so nicely in the leaf the designs tend to vary
light on
substance next to the pine the weeping willow at first I thought
one pine and then it was two every frame limitless you want to crop

boards nailed together to make fence a stern clarity akin to genius

enclosure three

firmly blanched in the somebody happening among
    the bargains opening a muscular trend
        what to make of damages so much stew in the mulling
always a context exclaiming or otherwise questioning or looking
                elsewhere
        damages opened the door it wasn't just shadow
this time the inescapable itness you think something to examine
is always your due you would lust after you would lust you would
as far as it goes and there's more at supper the preparations
set on the mark
messages in the air the face seen through suffering what's reflected
everybody started cheating and became that obvious
except the crooning we so much enjoyed it was morning overlooking
as it did the roofs one blue roof among so many colors I can't
remember but the blue roof light blue and baby blue roof

enclosure four

light ordinary in detail more lush hands
                  upon hand and within achieve so clearly
a shaking hither a reverb in glitter of neighborhood just door
a glance within
the next said and understood
tomorrow as discreet and aspired
chains rattled you didn't know face as such what kept me now I
see what kept me looking at all this time
undeniably you brought it all with you together at the carnival
                        we chose synonyms with care and later we
                            said statue with a flourish we know
for certain and along kept coming fog bundled carefully
divided into bones
that's close without saving the outcome where I began some
discoveries remain

enclosure five

no longer the broken branch with background summaries space time
cloud eye strung wires at onset
proportionate obstacles going staves off all day rooftops' harbinger
in fashion
acquaint like routine
perplexed horizon wave upon wave jumped up in sudden falling from
shoulders
one red shoe by the door caught the endless preparations
                            phases out the upcoming
                    by virtue the homestretch touch of chill plaudits
                                          the update
it was go around sudden at the root both yesterday and you
              left candles in a series of lost interests

enclosure six

surveying the composition
telescope in wide appeal came and went
shoebox beneath the freshly built stairs
                attitude crept through the tall and swaying
                                    another day older
communing via names reeked distance
                busily a-figuring cracks in the ice upon
cunning water trough
                          mane shook wind

sunlight in one corner particular and empty

enclosure seven

where met upon years
the later abstracted unchanged appearance
muscles brought in of remainder
discussed and quantum-ed dug up in greeting
walked easily with the long glad
brought two ways on the journey brought touch
brought story with tea brought crumbles
brought the non-born that lives and is buried
cat meows is fed furniture arrives and is placed
the same comments when passed on the street
and it goes on casual like you know accepted
in the justness the in fact I mean and is likely
yet beware the wreck in the sky
duplications how come it keeps coming back
better to strut you got the ways and means better
ease back into the timing better than space

enclosure eight

repetition encouraged break upon the long last
                    collect the reasonable   outlasted was it
the bread rose at dawn   consuming street toward street
                                      toward dunes
                        hopeful on the wing betwixt
                                    the silk bemused
                                    the silk touched
the warm and environ what else goggled on the slope was it upward
           a quick look was all taken back a sense of it always
               in my pocket it's what kept me glued sociably at tea
the weather perfect and in cement

enclosure nine

absence leads the investigation suddenly lit by
syllables   a coming impairment   flesh upon it
all   a bundling turned elsewhere   breathless is
nothing   that's where we get it   a beginning looks
out the upstairs window   the obvious taken this far
orchestral traffic felt timely and choice   oblivion hands
shadow multiplied in weight upcoming mindful
and possible   endless distinctions read from a book daily
aghast at summary   clothing assumed proportions   what's
not what was   that's where we get it   hello no longer steams
along   prepare for the ceremony   orchestral traffic felt timely
and choice   the attention paid   endless distinctions full of
reaches coming in gull-like   consequence at the site   the familiar
is vision   hopeful for rain sullen and perfect

enclosure ten

punctual as the wet brick   the latch on the gate
                                      falling measurably
the memorial has its place   obvious conclusions have drawn me
                                                    on before
shadow more than once the curve around which I have travelled
yours or whose claim on the other hand rises
that's it past like or simply taken on the big as if goes
straighter than wonder   possibly more heart filling out the
                                              obscure and tenuous
              who would have thought the rose would be so tedious
held up against bright lights against distance against others
who know or have known
                        the admission however was without cost

enclosure eleven

having circular without realizing the reach
    a bit of memory
        tossed about unfolded without picture
                      askance like this yes
          called to it   sound to it
obscurely partaking beneath dour boughs
long walk up the library stairs
burst of applause enclosed all else
transcendent cause thrashed about storm-like
called to wait   called the peremptory caller
        still a margin if we cared

enclosure twelve

dismay hasn't taken up the operation quite as total
as lastly met on the stairs   a bigness perseveres
in the costly and flickers   drought occupies or is
attention to have thought   a whistling on the crossed
street fully   a name I don't know   people cross one
another a movement purpose   agreements long out at sea
    banking hours kept us clued in reading signs signing
one upon another again a long sodden clasp up and at it
longer   sunglasses upon the invoice well described and
                                                                        totalled

IMAGO

can tell
a waltz from
a distance

the makings
a decision
or a stretch of time

x resulting
from collapse
of parallel lines

*

the past
until now
the roar before

you've heard
before